Guide To Ge~

With Examination of Conscience

Introduction

This is compiled from several good Catholics sources as an aid to making a General Confession and examining one's conscience. Several different examinations are included to help make good thorough confessions. Fr. Faber says that it is good to make new starts. And it is good sometimes to shake the spiritual life up and to look at ourselves from another angle. At the end is a format for making a Spiritual Confession, when we are unable to confess to a "duly authorized priest", as the Catechism tells us. To absolve us from our sins a man must not only be a priest, but he must be a priest of God authorized by the Catholic Church to absolve us from our sins, as the Council of Trent teaches us.

Included here are instructions on how to make a good general confession. Also there are many things useful for regular confessions. We have added a 'spiritual confession' for use when one cannot confess and instructions on the dispositions to make a Perfect Act of Contrition.

We hope these instructions compiled from the Saints and other holy sources will help all come into full conformity with the will of God. We also ask you to pray for us.

Saint Pius X Press

Fr. Leonard Goffine comments: "The literal meaning of this is the evil enemy, who some times so torments those whom he possesses that they lose the power of speech; in a spiritual sense, we may understand it to mean the shame which the devil takes away from the sinner, when he commits the sin, but gives back again, as false shame, before confession, so that the sinner conceals the sin, and thereby falls deeper.

"Be not ashamed to confess to one man," says St. Augustine, "that which you were not ashamed to do with one, perhaps, with many." Consider these words of the same saint: "Sincere confession subdues vice, conquers the evil one, shuts the door of hell, and opens the gates of paradise."

General Confession

A general confession is a repetition of the confessions of your whole life or of a certain part of it.

"A general confession", says St. Francis de Sales, "is for the majority of Christians a necessary means of salvation. It gives us a more complete knowledge of ourselves; it fills us with a wholesome shame at the sight of our sins; it relieves our mind of much anxiety and gives peace to our conscience; it excites in us good resolutions; it shows us God's wonderful patience and mercy towards us; it enables our confessor to direct us more safely; and, finally, it so dilates our heart, that we are ever after able to make our confession with greater confidence."

The inestimable advantages of a general confession are best appreciated at the hour of death, that dreadful moment, on which a whole eternity depends, — when the soul is about to be summoned before the tribunal of the Supreme Judge. Let us hearken to our divine Redeemer's warning: "Watch ye and be ye ready, for . . . the Lord of that servant shall come in a day that he hopeth not, and at an hour that he knoweth not" (Mat. 24, 42 44 50).

A man came one day to a priest to make a general confession. He said: "Am I not to die? After a life like mine I cannot die in peace, unless I make a general confession. If I put it off till my last illness, I shall hardly be able to make it at all. My bodily pains, my worldly affairs and the thoughts of my family will so distract me, that I shall scarcely be able to think of my soul. I must therefore make a good general confession while I have the time and the ability to do so."

If then, dear Christian, you find that a general confession is not only useful, but even necessary, do not put it off. Make it at once and make it well. When you lie down tonight think that this night may be your last, and say to yourself: "Were I now on my deathbed, what would I wish to have done?" Do not let the devil deceive you with the vain pretext that you have no time, that it is too difficult for you now to make a general confession, or that you will be better able to do so later. All such pretexts and delays only endanger your eternal salvation.

For whom is a General Confession necessary?

It is necessary for all adults who have never been to confession, and for all those whose confessions are sacrilegious.

He who has never made a good confession, must make a confession of his whole life.

He who has made sacrilegious confessions during only a part of his life, must confess since his last good confession.

1. He makes a bad confession who, through fear, shame or malice, willfully conceals or essentially misrepresents a mortal sin, or the number of his mortal sins.

2. He who, through sheer carelessness in his examen of conscience, omitted a mortal sin, or who purposely confessed any of his mortal sins in such a way as not to be understood by the confessor; he who chooses a confessor because he is deaf, or does not understand his language, and therefore cannot properly question him and give him the necessary admonitions.

3. He who will not give up the immediate occasion of sin.

4. He makes a bad confession who confesses his sins without supernatural sorrow, or without the firm purpose of avoiding sin and the proximate occasion of sin.

5. He makes a bad confession who does not sincerely intend to restore, as far as possible, the property or good name of his neighbor.

6. He who will not be reconciled with his enemy and sincerely forgive him.

7. He makes a bad confession who does not renounce forbidden secret societies, and he who is ignorant of the principal mysteries of faith, or who, through his fault, knows little or nothing of the Commandments of God and of the Church, the nature of the Sacraments he receives, and the necessary duties of his state of life.

All these classes of penitents are unworthy of absolution. If they receive absolution, it is worthless and sacrilegious in the sight of God. They are bound, under pain of eternal damnation, to make all such confessions over again.

For whom is a General Confession useful?

1 It is useful for such as wish to begin a new life, and to serve God more faithfully and fervently. Experience teaches that many Christians, after a good general confession, lead fervent and virtuous lives.

2. It is very useful for those who are about to marry, or to enter the religious or the ecclesiastical state, or to assume an important office, or to undertake a dangerous journey.

3. It is useful for all who wish to make a serious preparation for death.

A general confession is one of the best means of securing peace of conscience and preparing for a happy eternity. Many good Christians make every year a review or general confession. It makes them more humble, and preserves them from falling again and again into the same sins.

Those who are unreasonably scrupulous should not make a general confession without the express sanction of their confessor. They should obey him like good children and make frequent acts of contrition, and refrain from excessive examination of their conscience.

Examination Of Conscience For A General Confession

PRAYER: O Lord, help me to remember my sins, so that I can be sorry for them and root out their cause and resolve to sin no more. Amen.

Previous Questions. How long ago did you make your last confession? Did you receive absolution? Have you performed your penance? Did you willfully conceal a mortal sin, or confess without true sorrow, without firm purpose of amendment, or without intending to perform your penance? Did you, after this bad confession, go to Holy Communion? How many such sacrilegious confessions and Communions have you made? Have you also during that time received Confirmation, Extreme Unction, or the Sacrament of Matrimony?

Commandments Of God And The Precepts Of The Church

The Holy Cure of Ars states: "The commandments of God are the guides which God gives us to show us the road to heaven; like the names written up at the corners of the streets and on guideposts, to point out the way."

First Commandment: "I am the Lord thy God, thou shalt not have strange gods before Me." Luke 11:28: "Blessed are they that hear the word of God and keep it."

Have you denied the Catholic faith, openly rejected or spoken against any doctrine of the Catholic Church? — Have you disbelieved or willfully indulged in doubts against any article of faith, or suggested or encouraged such doubts in others? Have you betrayed the Catholic faith by saying that all religions are good, that a man may be saved in one as well as in another? How many times have you been guilty of these sins?

Have you read the Protestant Bible, heretical tracts or books, or sold, or lent them? Have you attended, or joined in false worship? Have you watched or listened to *radio preachers* on TV, radio or the Internet? Have you played or sung in places of false worship? Have you listened to heretical or infidel preachers or lecturers? How many times

Have you exposed your faith to danger by evil associations? Have you joined any secret society forbidden by the Church? Do you still belong to it? Have you, through your own fault, remained ignorant of the doctrines and duties of your religion? Have you remained a long time, a whole month, or longer, without reciting any prayer, or performing any act of devotion towards God? Have you sinned in a holy place, the church, the graveyard? Have you been guilty of great irreverence in church, by immodest conversation; by an unbecoming way of dressing, or by other gross misconduct? How many times?

Have you consulted fortune-tellers, whether in person, by phone or on the internet, or made use of superstitious practices, love potions, charms, etc.; read, kept, given, lent or sold dream-books, fortune-telling books, and the like? Have you attended or taken part in spiritualist meetings, and the like? How many times have you been guilty of these sins?

Second Commandment: "Thou shalt not take the Name of the Lord thy God in vain." If we mean what we say in the "Our Father, "Hallowed be Thy Name", it would be impossible to be careless with the Name of God. In 1846 when the Blessed Virgin appeared at LaSalette She said in part, "Those who drive carts cannot speak without putting the Name of My Son in the middle"

Have you been guilty of blasphemy by angry, injurious, or insulting words against God or any of His perfections? Have you murmured against God; — said He was unjust, cruel, etc.? Did you even hate God? Did you sin and remain in sin because God is good? Have you given way to despair? To presumption? — Have you pronounced in a blasphemous or irreverent manner, or in anger, the holy name of God, the name of Jesus Christ, or that of any of the saints? Spoken in a blasphemous manner of sacred things, or abused the words of Holy Scripture by any indecent or grossly irreverent application? How many times! Have you watched movies or television where blasphemy was used?

Have you sworn falsely? — Done so to the prejudice of your neighbor? — Taken rash, foolish or sinful oaths? — Joined an oath-bound secret society? How many oaths did you take in that society? Did you take an oath to be revenged or to commit some other crime? Have you broken a lawful oath? Induced others to swear falsely or unnecessarily, or to break a lawful oath? How often? Have you cursed yourself or your neighbor? Did you mean it? Is this sin habitual? How often do you curse in the day? Have you made any rash vows? Have you broken or neglected a lawful vow, or changed it without permission? How often? Have you broken a promise of marriage without sufficient cause?

Third Commandment of God and the Precepts of the Church: Remember thou keep holy the Sabbath Day. In 1846 when the Blessed Virgin appeared at LaSalette She said in part, "I gave you six days for work, I kept the seventh for Myself and no one wishes to give it to Me.

Have you been habitually absent from the sermons and instructions? Have you kept the Lord's Day holy? How often have you performed unnecessary servile work on Sundays and other Holydays of Obligation, or caused others to do so? (Do you know what the Holydays of Obligation are?) How often have you desecrated these days by frequenting ungodly company, by sinful amusements, gambling, immodest dancing, immoral movies or television, or drinking to excess?

How often have you without necessity eaten meat or caused others to eat meat on days of abstinence? How often have you broken the laws of fasting? Have you been married before a civil magistrate, or even before a heretical preacher? Have you, without dispensation, married a relative or an unbaptized person? Have you contracted marriage in any way forbidden by the Church?

Fourth Commandment: "Honor thy father and thy mother"

"If anyone has not care of his own, and especially of those of his house, he is worse than an infidel." I Timothy5:8

"Character in parents is terribly important because of the influence it exerts." Sins of the Parents, page 172

Saint John Vianney: "A father and mother can serve God by bringing up their children as good Christians."

"Praise not any man before death, for a man is known by his children." Ecclesiasticus 11:30

Have you despised or even hated your parents, wished their death, or that some other misfortune should befall them? Have you insulted, mocked, ridiculed or cursed them? Have you threatened them, or even lifted your hand to strike them? How often have you been guilty of such sins?

Have you disobeyed them in serious matters; kept bad company, read bad books and papers, and so on? Have you sorely grieved your parents by your ingratitude, or misconduct? Have you, still a minor, promised or even contracted marriage without their knowledge? Have you neglected or refused to aid them in their wants? Have you been ashamed of them on account of their poverty? Have you faithfully accomplished their last will? Have you neglected to pray for them? Have you neglected to pray for the repose of their souls?

Have you been disrespectful and disobedient to your spiritual superiors, the bishops and priests of the Church? Have you behaved towards them in a haughty and insulting manner? Have you taken part with the disaffected and seditious? Have you neglected to contribute, according to your means, to the support of your pastor and church? Have you resisted the lawful authorities of the country, or taken part in any mob, or association to commit deeds of violence, or disturb the public peace? How many times?

Fifth Commandment: "Thou shalt not kill." "It is also a sin willfully to produce any serious illness, by eating to excess, or by eating food injurious to health; for we are bound to preserve our life, and to avoid all danger of death." Saint Alphonsus in his Catechism.

Have you by act, participation, instigation, counsel, or consent, been guilty of anyone's death or bodily injury? Have you intended or attempted to take another's life? How often have you committed these sins? How often have you intended or attempted to take your own life? Have you injured your health by excess in eating or drinking? Have you been drunk or been the cause of drunkenness in others? Have you taken harmful drugs, whether prescribed by a physician or acquired illegally? Have you taken these drugs to become intoxicated? Have you induced a doctor to prescribe addictive drugs for you? How many times have you been guilty of these sins?

Have you by act, advice or consent, done anything to hinder, or to destroy life? How often? Have you wished the death of your neighbor, or that some other misfortune should befall him? Have you intended or attempted to injure, or ill-treat others? How often? Have you been at enmity with your neighbor? Have you refused to speak to him or salute him? How often? Are you now reconciled with him? How often have you excited others to anger or revenge? Have you through avarice, passion or revenge, engaged in vexatious or unjust lawsuits?

Have you harmed the soul of anyone by giving scandal? Have you, by wicked words, deeds or bad example, ruined innocent persons, taught them bad habits or things they should not know? Have you thrown temptation in the way of the weak? Have you tried to dissuade or discourage those who were willing to repent and reform? How often have you been guilty of these sins? Have you neglected to give alms according to your means, or to relieve those in distress?

Sixth And Ninth Commandments: "Thou shalt not commit adultery" and "Thou shalt not covet thy neighbors wife." "O my children, if there were not some pure souls here and there, to make amends to the good God, and disarm His justice, you would see how we would be punished! For now, this crime is so common in the world, that it is enough to make one tremble. One may say, my children, that hell vomits forth its abominations upon the earth, as the chimneys of the steam-engine vomit forth smoke." The Cure of Ars

These commandments forbid everything that is contrary to purity. Every sin of this nature, whether in deed, word, or even thought, when willful and deliberate, is a mortal sin and must be confessed.

How often have you dwelt with willful pleasure on impure thoughts or imaginations, or consented to them in your heart? Have you willfully desired to see or do anything impure? Have you watched immoral movies or television? Have you visited immoral websites?

How often have you made use of impure language, allusions, or words of double meaning? How many were listening to you? Have you listened with willful pleasure to immodest language? How often have you sung immodest songs or listened to them? How often have you boasted of your sins? How often have you read immoral books or papers, or lent or sold them to others? How often have you written, sent or received improper letters or messages? How often have you gazed with willful pleasure on improper objects, images or cards, or shown them to others?

How often have you voluntarily exposed yourself to the occasion of sin by sinful curiosity; by frequenting dangerous company, places, or dangerous or sinful amusements; by immodest dances and indecent plays; by remaining alone in company with those of the other sex, or by undue familiarities? Do you keep sinful company now? Did you ruin an innocent person? How long have you been addicted to secret sins? How often did you commit them? How often have you been guilty of improper liberties with others? How far have you carried your sinful conduct? How often have you by your freedom of manners, your immodest dress, and so on, been the cause of temptation to others?

Have you been guilty of seduction, or even rape? Did you accomplish your designs by a false promise of marriage? Have you refused to repair the injury done? Have you committed crimes against nature? Have you taken part in the sins of others? You must mention those circumstances that change the nature of your sin — the sex, the relationship and the condition — whether married, single or bound by vow. Were you married or single at the time?

Seventh And Tenth Commandments: "Thou shalt not steal" and "Thou shalt not covet thy neighbors goods." St. Ambrose: "He who spends too much is a robber."

Have you stolen money or anything of value? Is it still in your possession? What was its value? How much did you take each time? How often? Throughout this whole examination you must not merely tell the number of sins, you must also tell, as nearly as possible, the value of what you took, or the amount of damage caused by your injustice, that the confessor may know whether your sins are mortal or not, and what restitution you have to make.

Have you stolen anything consecrated to God, or from a holy place? This is a sacrilege.

Have you charged exorbitant prices, or made out false bills, or cheated in the weight, measure, quantity or quality of your goods? Have you cheated in games? Have you been in the habit of gambling, and to what extent? Have you engaged in deceitful speculations or enterprises to the injury of the simple and unwary? Have you defrauded your creditors? Have you entered into debts you knew you could not repay? Have you been guilty of forgery or swindling? Have you charged interest? Have you robbed the poor? Have you passed counterfeit or mutilated money? Have you been guilty of bribery, of taking bribes?

Have you kept things you found without inquiring for the owner? Have you retained any of the money intrusted to you? Have you failed to return things borrowed? Have you neglected to pay your debts? Have you contracted debts without any reasonable hope of paying?

Have you bought, received, or concealed things you knew to be stolen? Have you been the cause of ruin or damage to the property of another? Allowed your cattle to injure the neighbor's crop, etc.? Have you squandered the money of your husband, wife, parents, etc. in buying costly dresses, jewelry, in drinking, etc?

Have you been careless of goods intrusted to your charge? Have you received pay for work or service you never did, or done it so poorly that it had to be done over again?

Have you sought to gain your cause by bribery, threats, or other unjust means? Have you set fire to your property and pocketed the insurance money? Have you, in your dealings, taken advantage of the simple, the young and inexperienced? Have you made hard bargains with the poor, or those in distress? Have you been guilty of fraud or embezzlement in any public office or private trust? Have you caused any injury, or loss by your negligence or culpable ignorance in the discharge of your profession or employment? Have you in any way taken part in another's theft, fraud, usury, or injustice? Have you concealed the injustice of others, when it was your duty to report?

Have you attempted, or intended, or willfully desired to rob, steal, defraud, or commit any kind of injustice? Have you, by calumny or other unjust means, caused anyone to lose his situation? Did you vote for anyone you knew to be unfit for office? Examine whether you have repaired all the injustice you have done. Your sins will not be pardoned so long as you refuse or willfully neglect to make restitution. If what you have unjustly acquired is no longer in your possession, return the value of it. If you cannot restore the whole, restore at least a part, and that without delay. If you are unable to restore at once, you must have the firm and sincere resolution to do so as soon as possible. You must also strive earnestly to acquire the means of doing so. The obligation of restitution is binding until it is fully discharged. Restitution must be made to the owner. If the owner cannot be found, you must give the money to God, that is, to the poor, the Church, or some charitable purpose.

Have you been envious of the goods of others? Of their luxuries? Have your gone into debt to obtain similar luxuries for yourself?

Eighth Commandment: "Thou shalt not bear false witness" especially against thyself.

Have you taken a false oath or advised others to do so? Have you signed false papers or documents or forged any writings? What injury have you done thereby? How often have you committed these sins? Have you been guilty of malicious lying? Have you put in circulation, or repeated any scandalous report, you knew or believed to be false? Have you been guilty of detraction in serious matters, by making known your neighbor's secret sins or defects? Have you watched TV, listened to radio or visited internet sites where detraction is indulged in? Have you done anything to blacken his character or injure his interests? Have you caused ill feeling between others by tale bearing? Have you revealed an important secret? Did you without authority read another's letters? How often, and in presence of how many persons, have you committed these Sins?

Have you endeavored to repair the harm you have done, by contradicting your false reports? Have you tried honestly to restore the good name that you have injured? Have you spoken against the priest, bishop or anyone consecrated to God? This is a sacrilege.

How often have you been guilty of unjust suspicions and rash judgments?

The Particular Duties Of Your State

Parents. Have you always taken proper care of the life and health of your children! Have you exposed them to great danger before their birth? Have you placed them in your own bed where they were in danger of being suffocated? Have you failed to provide for their needs? Have you given them proper food, clothing, etc.? Have you even deserted them! Have you endeavored to procure them a good and Christian education according to your means? Did you teach them a trade or profession, so that they could gain an honest livelihood? Have you manifested an unjust preference for one to the prejudice of the others? Have you been neglectful, unkind and even cruel to your children, stepchildren or wards? Have you placed television or other unimportant activities in front of the needs of your children and spouse? (See stat on TV watching below)

Have you forced your children into a state of life, for which they had no vocation? Have you hindered them from following their vocation to the religious or ecclesiastical state? Have you, without reasonable cause, opposed their inclinations with regard to marriage?

Have you neglected the care of their salvation? Have you failed to teach them their prayers? Have you neglected to inspire them, in their tender years, with the love of God and a horror of Sin? Have you delayed their baptism too long? Have you neglected to have them prepared and brought at the proper age to Confession, holy Communion and Confirmation? Have you neglected their religious instruction, or sent them to heretical or godless schools? Have you failed to obtain the dispensation necessary for using non-Catholic courses and the precautions prescribed by the Church? Have you failed to take them to Mass on Sundays and Holydays? Have you failed to keep the Lord's Day holy with your children? Have you caused them to observe abstinence on the days prescribed? Have you placed them in a situation where they could not practice their religion, or where their faith or their virtue was in danger? Have you exposed their innocence to danger by letting the

13

different sexes sleep together, or by keeping them at night in your own bedroom? Have you allowed your children to watch improper movies or television? Did you watch with them or encourage them to watch?

Have you watched over their conduct carefully? Have you seen where they spend their time, with what companions they associate, and if they are addicted to any secret vice? Have you allowed them to wander where they would? Have you intrusted them to the care of servants that were irreligious or of loose morals? Have you allowed them to read love stories, trashy novels and other dangerous books? Have you allowed them to take part in sinful or dangerous amusements? Have you allowed them free intercourse with persons of the other sex; to receive visits alone, at improper hours, or to stay out late at night? Have you allowed immodest dances in your house?

Have you failed to correct and punish them when they deserved it? Have you allowed them to curse or use improper language without chastising them? Have you, through indifference or misguided affection, left them without restraint? Or have you, on the contrary, cursed them in anger; treated them brutally, or exasperated or scandalized them by violent language, abusive names, etc.? Have you scandalized them by bad example, by neglecting your religion?

The Married. Did you enter the marriage state from base and unchristian motives? Have you by your giddy conduct been the cause of jealousy and grief to your companion? Have you profaned the sanctity of matrimony by misuse, by overstepping the bounds of Christian modesty, or by trying to hinder its lawful end? Have you sinned against each other by angry words, opprobrious names, or even by quarrels and blows? How often have you been guilty of these sins?

Have you, without just cause and lawful permission, abandoned your companion in life, lived separate or remained long absent?

Husbands. Have you been faithless to your marriage vows? Have you treated your wife in a gross, cruel or tyrannical manner, beat her, or abused her in your anger? Have you made her unhappy by your coldness, stinginess, neglect and unfeeling conduct, or by spending your leisure time away from home or in front of the TV or computer? Have you treated her with attention and forbearance, when she was in a delicate condition? Have you compelled her to act against her conscience, to sin against the laws of nature? Have you neglected to support your wife and children? Have you squandered your earnings or the property of your wife?

Wives. Have you, unknown to your husband, made useless and extravagant expenses for yourself or relatives? How much? Have you caused discord by your selfishness and jealousy and by your unfriendly conduct towards his relatives? Have you broken your marriage vows? Have you given rise to jealousy by your levity; by trying to win the admiration and affection of others? Have you been respectful and obedient to him in all things reasonable and lawful? Have you made home disagreeable by your ill temper, scolding and faultfinding, or by pretended or imaginary ailments? Have you without just cause refused him his marriage rights? Have you induced him to offend God and act contrary to the laws of nature? How often have you been guilty of these sins? Have you done your part towards the support of the family, or have you, on the contrary, been idle and neglectful of your household duties?

Employees and Servants. Have you served your employers diligently and faithfully? Have they suffered any harm or loss through your fault, neglect or wastefulness? Have you retained part of what they gave you to make purchases, or taken anything under pretence that your wages were too low? How much? How often? Have you concealed from them the theft or misconduct of your fellow-employee in matters pertaining to your charge? Have you revealed unnecessarily the faults of your employers, sowed discord in their families, or been the cause, by false or malicious complaints, of other employees being discharged? Are you in a situation where your faith or morals are endangered, or where you have not the opportunity of fulfilling your religious duties? Have you connived at or aided your employers in their crimes? Did you print, bind, or sell books or papers against faith or morals? Did you sell immoral or irreligious movies, TV programs, computer programs, etc.?

How to Deal With Your Predominant Fault

We all have a habit of sin or sins, which we must deal with. We all have a weakness in one place or another and this is the most difficult battle. This 'cross of sin' has to be crucified and removed from our life. Let us consider the following points: Do you as far as possible, make this fault, or its opposite virtue, the subject of your particular examen every evening? Are you constant and earnest in your efforts to overcome the difficulties which you meet with in this combat? Are you careful to humble yourself for your faults, and to give a faithful account of them? Are your faults as frequent as those of the previous month?

Examination of Conscience
Based on the Seven Deadly Sins

Pride

"**Pride** is an untrue opinion of ourselves, an untrue idea of what we are not.", Saint John Vianney.

Proverbs 16:5 "Every proud man is an abomination to the Lord:"

Ecclesiasticus 10:15: "Pride is the beginning of all sin."

Thus Pride is conquered by humility.

Have I a superior attitude in thinking, or speaking or acting? Am I snobbish?

Have I offensive, haughty ways of acting or carrying myself?

Do I hold myself above others? Do I demand recognition?

Do I desire to be always first? Do I seek advice?

Am I ready to accept advice? Am I in any sense a "bully"?

Am I inclined to be "bossy"?

Am I prone to belittle persons, or places, or things?

Am I prone to be critical of persons, places, things?

Do I speak ill of others?

Have I lied about others?

Do I make known the faults of others?

Am I ready to speak about the faults of others? Do I find fault easily?

Do I seek to place the blame on others, excusing myself?

Am I quick to see the faults of others? Do I ridicule others?

Is there anyone to whom I refuse to speak? Is there anyone to whom I have not spoken for a long time?

Am I prone to argue? Am I positive and offensive in my arguments? Have I a superior, "a know-it-all attitude" in arguments?

Am I self-conscious?

Does human respect enter into my daily life?

Am I sensitive? Am I easily wounded?

Envy

"**Envy** is a sadness which we feel, on account of the good that happens to our neighbor.", Saint John Vianney.

Wisdom 2:24-25: "By the envy of the devil, death came into the world: and they follow him that are on his side."

Envy is conquered by brotherly love.

Do I feel sad at the prosperity of others? At their success in games? In athletics?

Do I rejoice at their failures?

Do I envy the riches of others?

Father Faber gives the following rules for the practice of fraternal charity:

1. Often reflect on some good point in each of your brethren.

2. Reflect on the opposite faults in yourself.

3. Do this most in the case of those whom you are most inclined to criticize.

4. Never claim rights, or even let ourselves feel that we have them, as this spirit is most fatal to obedience and charity.

5. Charitable thoughts are the only security for charitable deeds and words. They save us from surprises, especially from surprises of temper.

6. Never have an aversion for another, much less manifest it.

7. Avoid particular friendships.

8. Never judge another. Always, if possible, excuse the faults we see, and if we cannot excuse the action, excuse the intention. We cannot all think alike, and we should, therefore, avoid attributing bad motives to others.

Sloth

"**Sloth** is a kind of cowardice and disgust, which makes us neglect and omit our duties, rather than do violence to discipline ourselves.", Saint John Vianney, "We will not discipline ourselves; we wilt not put ourselves to any inconvenience. Everything makes us tired, everything revolts the slothful person. ... 0 my children! how miserable we are in losing, in this way, the time that we might so usefully employ in gaining heaven, in preparing ourselves for eternity!"

"Since base slothful spirits given over to external pleasures are neither used to combat nor trained in spiritual arms, they rarely preserve charity and usually let themselves suffer a mortal blow. This happens more easily because by venial sin the soul has been prepared for mortal sin.", Saint Francis de Sales.

Ecclesiasticus 33:29: "For idleness has taught much evil."
Sloth is conquered by diligence and fervour in the service of God.

Have I an inordinate love of rest, neglecting my duties?
Do I act lazily?
Am I too fond of rest?
Do I take lazy positions in answering prayers? Do I kneel in a lounging way?
Do I delight in idle conversation?
Am I fervent in the service of God?

"There are three ways of being idle: doing nothing whatever; doing evil; doing other things than the duties of our position in life and its office require, or if this work is done without a good intention, or not from the love of God."   Goffine, 'The Church's Year' Instruction for Septuagesima Sunday.
"Three-quarters of those who are Christians labor for nothing but to satisfy the body, which will soon be buried and corrupted, while they do not give a thought to their poor soul, which must be happy or miserable for all eternity. They have neither sense nor reason: it makes one tremble. ... Good Christians, who labor to save their souls and to work out their salvation, are always happy and contented; they enjoy beforehand the happiness of heaven: they will be happy for all eternity." Saint John Vianney.

'Particular Examen' by James F. McElhone, C.S.C. 1952 Page 125: "Too many people are satisfied with mediocrity."

"No time must be lost, but every moment must be employed in prayer, in reading or in performing the duties of your state of life." Saint Alphonsus.
"Nothing is so precious as time; and yet comes it that nothing is so little valued? Men will spend hours in jesting, or standing at the window (or sitting in front of the TV) or in the middle of the road, to see what passes; and if you ask them what they are doing, they will tell you they are passing away the time. O time, now so much despised! you will be of all things the most valued by such persons when death will have surprised them What will they not be willing to give for one hour of so much lost time! But time will no longer be available to them, when it is said to each of them: 'Go forth, Christian soul, out of this world:' hurry to

be gone, for now there is no more time for you. How they will holler, sadly Alas! I have wasted my whole life; during so many years I might have become a saint; but how far I am from being one; and shall I become one now, now that there is no more time for me! But to what purpose will such lamentations be, when the dying man is on the verge of that moment on which eternity depends?" Saint Alphonsus.

Covetousness

"**Covetousness** is an disordered love of the goods of this world.", Saint John Vianney.

Proverbs 30:8-9: "Remove far from me vanity, and lying words. Give me neither beggary or riches: give me only the necessaries of life: Lest perhaps being filled, I should tempted to deny, and say: Who is the Lord? or being compelled by poverty, I should steal, and foreswear the name of my God."

Covetousness is conquered by liberality.

Do I dispose of my money properly or selfishly?
Do I discharge my duties in justice to my fellow man?
Do I discharge my duties in justice to the Church?

Gluttony

"**Gluttony** is a disordered love of eating and drinking.", Saint John Vianney.

Ecclesiasticus 37:34: "By excess many have perished: but he that is temperate, shall prolong life."

Ecclesiasticus 31:23: "Watching and diseases are with the intemperate man."

Gluttony is conquered by abstinence.

Do I *eat to live* or *live to eat*?

Do I drink to excess? Do I get drunk?

Do I misuse prescription drugs?

Do I use *illegal drugs*?

Have I allowed myself to become addicted to alcohol and/or drugs?

Lust

"**Lust** is the love of the pleasures that are contrary to purity.", Saint John Vianney.

I Corinthians 15:33: "Be not led astray, evil communications corrupt good manners."

Please see the Sixth and Ninth Commandments.

Lust is conquered by chastity.

Anger

"**Anger** is an emotion of the soul, which leads us violently to repel whatever hurts or displeases us.", Saint John Vianney "This emotion, my children, comes from the Devil: it shows that we are in his hands: that he is the master of our heart: that he holds all the strings of it, and makes us dance as he pleases.", Saint John Vianney

Ecclesiasticus 27:33: "Anger and fury are both of them abominable, and the sinful man shall be subject to them."

Matthew 5:22: "But I say to you, that whosoever is angry with his brother, shall be in danger of the judgement. ... And whosoever shall say, Thou fool, shall be in danger of hell fire."

Anger is conquered by patience.

Am I prone to anger?

Does practically any little thing arouse me to temper?

Am I what is generally termed "a sore-head"? Do I repress the first signs of anger? Do I strive to get along well with everybody? Do I ponder over slights or injuries and even presume them?

Do I rejoice at the misfortunes of others? Do I think of means of revenge? Of "getting even"?

Am I of an argumentative disposition? Have I a spirit of contradiction?

Am I given to ridicule of persons, places, or things?

Am I hard to get along with?

Do I carry grudges, remain "on the outs" with anyone?

Do I talk about the faults of others?

Do I reveal the faults or defects of others?

Do I reveal the faults of others from the wrong motive?

"For we know him that hath said: Vengeance belongeth to me, and I will repay." (Hebrews 10:30)

When we seek revenge upon another, we are declaring by our actions that we are *god*. "For God doth know that in what day soever you shall eat thereof, your eyes shall be opened: **and you shall be as Gods**, knowing good and evil". (Genesis 3:5) Jesus tells us not only to love our friends, but also our enemies. We are supposed to love everyone **and do good to them and wish them well.** Some of us have a desire to *get even. You can't do that to ME.* And yet let us consider that we have wronged many and think little of it.

And anger can take many forms. Some may throw *fits* even the level of the mortal sin of destruction of property. Others refuse to salute their *enemy* or to help them in any way, when Jesus tells us to do the opposite. Some agitate all around them against their current *enemy*, by telling the *evil* their *enemy* has done to them. This is the sin of detraction, and if the story is embellished or even not true, then this is the sin of calumny. Detraction is to reveal the faults of another, whereas calumny is to attribute faults to another that he does not possess. Both are sins against the Eighth Commandment. A person's right to his good name remains, even if this is undeserved.

The only time we may reveal the faults of another are:

To tell his superior. For instance if we see a child misbehaving, we must inform his parents.

To warn someone of a clear and present danger. If we know that a man indulges in lust with every woman he dates and we know someone who is contemplating dating him, then we must warn her of the danger to her virtue. The same is true of a person who is in the habit of stealing from his employer; we must warn his prospective employer.

A Short Examination of Conscience

Sins Against The Ten Commandments

The First Commandment

Have you doubted in matters of faith? Consulted fortune-tellers? Believed in dreams? Made use of superstitious practices? Gone to places of false worship and taken an active part in the religious services of a false church? Belonged to Masons, Communists, of some other forbidden society? Read anti-Catholic books or papers? Neglected religious instruction? Omitted religious duties through fear or ridicule? Murmured against God, or despaired of His mercy? Have you rashly presumed on His goodness in committing sin? Did you pray in time of temptation? For your family? Have you neglected your daily prayers? Have you recited them carelessly, without devotion, thoughtlessly? Have you missed spending a reasonable amount of time in thanksgiving after Holy Communion? Have you been irreverent toward God, sacred persons, places or things? Have you associated with people who might have a bad influence upon your life? Have you refused to place signs of faith in your home, such as a crucifix, picture of the Blessed Mother or the saints?

The Second Commandment

Have you taken the name of God in vain? Laughed at the profane use of the name of God or irreverent speech by others? Given bad example to children by such speech in their presence, or by neglecting to correct a child when irreverent or profane language was used? Spoken disrespectfully of the saints or holy things? Allowed others in your household to do the same? Sworn falsely, that is, called upon God to witness the truth of what you were saying, when you were in reality telling a lie? Sworn rashly, or in slight and trivial matters? Have you cursed persons, animals, or things? Have you blasphemed, that is, used insulting language expressing contempt for God, His saints or sacred things? Have you caused others to do so? Have you criticized God's mercy or justice, or murmured against His providence?

The Third Commandment

Have you assisted at Mass on Sundays and Holydays? Have you been late for Mass? Behaved properly in Church? Have you performed or commanded unnecessary servile work, bought or sold without necessity, or in any other way - gambling, drinking - profaned these holy days?

The Fourth Commandment

Have you shown due honor, love, gratitude and obedience to your parents? Have you shown due honor and obedience to your pastors and other lawful superiors? Have you asked their pardon when you hurt them? Have you been disrespectful to your parents by speaking angrily to them, saying unkind, harsh words to them and about them, or by being ashamed of them? If you are a parent, have you shown this lack of honor, love and gratitude to your parents in the presence of your children? Have you criticized them and rejected some of their orders? Have you corrected and punished your children for serious transgressions, or forbidden them to enter serious occasions of sin? Have you cooperated with teachers in the education of your children? Have you refused to send your children to Catholic school when you could have done so and had no permission from bishop or pastor to do otherwise? If there is no Catholic school in your vicinity, have you sent your children to catechism faithfully? Have you taken an interest in their catechism lessons? Have you cooperated with the Pastor and the Sisters in the projects sponsored by them to stimulate the children's interest in the faith? Have you trained and corrected your children in regard to chastity? Have you been disrespectful to aged persons? Have you had proper care for children and those dependent on you - both in physical and religious matters? Above all, have you given them a good example? If you are a child, have you refused to speak to your father or mother? Have you resented them? Have you disobeyed your parents when they gave you orders to avoid bad companions or dangerous occasions to sin? Have you obeyed the rules they made concerning persons to be brought into the house, the hours to be kept at night, or the conduct within the home? When earning money, while living at home or while still subject to your parents, have you refused them part of your earnings when they needed it or demanded it? As a citizen, have you obeyed laws of the city and country made for the safety and well-being of all?

The Fifth Commandment

The fifth commandment forbids: Murder, suicide, criminal neglect that might cause serious injury or death to another, serious anger and hatred, abortion, mercy killing, the use of narcotics, sterilization, drunkenness, help extended to another to commit a mortal sin, fighting, anger, hatred and revenge. Have you procured, desired, or hastened the death of any one? Have you been guilty of anger, hatred, quarreling, revenge? Used provoking language, insulting words, ridicule? Refused to speak to others? Caused enmities? Given scandal? Did you eat or drink too much? Have you been unkind, irritable, impatient? Have you provoked others to anger offended them, hurt them by anger or impatience? Have you entertained thoughts of jealousy, revenge, aversion, resentment or contempt of others? Have you kept company with those who drink to excess? Have you encouraged them to drink? Have you jested about their drunkenness? Have you neglected your health or endangered your life? Have you neglected to take care of the health of your children or those subject to you? Have you endangered the life of others by driving an automobile while intoxicated or caused real danger to the safety of others in any other way?

The Sixth and Ninth Commandments
These two commandments demand purity and modesty in our life: in our thoughts, words, and actions, whether alone or with others. In general, these commandments forbid: adultery, fornication, self-abuse, indecent dressing, necking, impure kisses, impure dancing, impure talk, sins against nature, birth control, impure touches, petting, looking at impure pictures, dances, floor shows, movies, or reading impure books or magazines. Have you been guilty of impure or immodest thoughts, words or actions - alone or with others? Have you spoken words or phrases of double meaning? Have you told suggestive stories? Have you encouraged others to do so? Have you taught others to do this? Have you avoided occasions of sin in this matter? Have you guarded your sight, or allowed your eyes to wander in curiosity over obviously dangerous objects? Have you put yourself in an occasion of sin by reading bad books, looking at indecent pictures, keeping bad company, attending immoral performances, watching indecent movies or television programs, singing lewd songs, and the like? Have you distributed obscene books or magazines? Have you informed others of places of distribution? Have you encouraged others to read them? Have you desired to do impure things? Have you been an occasion of sin to others, by your conversation, dress, appearance, or actions? Have you touched yourself impurely? If you are married, have you committed sins of impurity with another married or single person? Taken part in prolonged kisses and embraces with others beside your partner in marriage? Have you used contraceptive means in performing marriage

duties? Have you, without good reason, refused or neglected to render the marriage obligation when seriously asked?

The Seventh and Tenth Commandments

These commandments forbid: robbery and burglary, graft, bribes, stealing and damaging the property of others. These commandments forbid not merely stealing but every type of dishonest dealing, such as, cheating, unjust keeping of what belongs to others, unjust damage to property of others, graft on the part of public officials. These commandments are also violated by merchants who use false weights, measures, who make exorbitant profits or lie about the essential qualities of their goods; by those who obtain money from others by persuading them to make unsound investments with the assurance of gain; by those who knowingly pass counterfeit money, or take undue advantage of the ignorance or necessity of another; by employers who defraud laborers; by employees who waste time during working hours, perform careless work or neglect to take reasonable care of the property of their employers; by employers who charge customers exorbitant prices; by those who do not return what they borrowed; by running up a charge account and not paying it; not returning found articles; selling articles with hidden defects for the usual price; not paying one's bills; by depriving one's family of necessities by gambling, drinking or foolish spending. Have you stolen or retained ill-gotten goods? Damaged or wasted the property of others? Accepted bribes? Neglected to make restitution, or to help the poor? Have you desired the goods of others? Squandered their goods? As a parent, have you taught your children a strict sense of honesty and justice, punishing any slight theft or deceit? Have you sinned in any way mentioned above?

The Eighth Commandment

This commandment forbids: lies, calumny, detraction, perjury, unjust and unnecessary criticism, fault-finding, gossip, backbiting, insults, rash judgment, the telling of secrets one is bound to keep, cheating, tale-bearing. Have you borne false witness for or against another? Been guilty of detraction, flattery, hypocrisy, lying, rash judgment? Have you entertained unkind thoughts of others? Have you harbored suspicions, nursed resentments, refused to forgive others when they expressed their contrition? Have you spread unkind remarks others make to you? Do you discuss the faults of your parents, wife, husband, children with others who have no business knowing anything about them? At home are you given to nagging, complaining, arguing, refusing to talk, calling names, petty quarreling? Have you brought any harm to your neighbor and have you tried to repair it, as far as you were able? Have you tried to destroy the good work performed by another, or to hinder it seriously? Have you been sensitive, hurt, cool, thoughtless with others?

Sins Against The Precepts Of The Church

I. Have you observed all Sundays and Holydays as commanded by the Church?

II. Have you kept the fast? Eaten meat on prohibited days? Encouraged others to violate the precepts of the Church? Scandalized others by your failure to obey the Church in this matter? Have you nibbled between meals?

III. Have you gone to confession at least once a year? Received Holy Communion during Easter Time?

IV. Are you a member of any forbidden society? Are you a Communist?

V. Have you contributed to the support of the Church, school, pastor? Have you prevented others from fulfilling this obligation? Have you fomented rebellion against proper Church authority? Have you given bad example to your children by refusing to support the Church? Have you tried to teach your children to give their share for the support of the Church? Have you ridiculed those who are doing their share and often times more than their share for the support of the Church?

VI. Have you married contrary to the laws of the Catholic Church, or aided others in doing so? Are you keeping such company that may some day prove dangerous for you and lead you to a violation of this precept of the Church? Are you encouraging others to keep such company?

Spiritual Confession

Fr. Demaris says (in 'They Have Taken Away My Lord'): "Nothing silences measures which are the tests of Saints, if we cannot confess our sins to priests, confess them to God." Indeed, the lack of the ability to present ourself before a priest of God, who is duly authorized by God's Church to hear our confession and to absolve us is one of the largest tests of the saints of these days. Indeed, Apocalypse is right when it tells us to have patience in these times. However, we must follow the advice of Saint Thomas Aquinas to do our part, when we cannot receive the Sacrament of Confession. We ask all to study the Catechism, especially on the matter of the perfect act of contrition, which will restore us to grace until we can fulfill our promise to confess our sins, which we make in the most well know Act of Contrition. Let us also consecrate our efforts to the restoration of the priesthood, so that we can again confess to the priest of God! The following prayers will assist us to make a formal spiritual confession.

Prayer to Implore the Divine Assistance to Make a Good Confession

O Almighty and most merciful God, Who has made me out of nothing, and redeemed me by the Precious Blood of Thine Only Son; Who has with so much patience borne with me to this day, notwithstanding all my sins and ingratitude; ever calling after me to return to Thee from the ways of vanity and iniquity, in which I have been quite wearied out in the pursuit of empty toys and mere shadows; seeking in vain to satisfy my thirst in unclean waters, and my hunger with husks of swine: behold, O most gracious Lord, I now sincerely desire to leave all these my evil ways, to forsake the region of death where I have so long lost myself, and to return to Thee, the Fountain of Life. I desire, like the prodigal son, to enter seriously into myself, and with the like resolution to arise without delay, and to go home to my Father – though I am most unworthy to be called His child – in hopes of meeting with the like reception from His most tender mercy. But, O my God, though I can go astray from Thee of myself, yet I cannot make one step towards returning to Thee, unless Thy divine grace move and assist me. This grace, therefore, I most humbly implore, prostate in spirit before the throne of Thy mercy; I beg it for the sake of Jesus Christ Thy Son,

Who died on the Cross for my sins; I know that Thou desirest not the death of a sinner, but that he may be converted and live; I know Thy mercies are above all Thy works; and I most confidently hope that as in Thy mercy Thou hast spared me so long, and hast now given me this desire of returning to Thee, so Thou wilt finish the work which Thou hast begun, and bring me to a perfect reconciliation with Thee.

I desire now to comply with Thy holy institution of the Sacrament of Penance; I desire to confess my sins with all sincerity to Thee and to Thy minister; and therefore I desire to know myself, and to call myself to account by a diligent examination of my conscience. Since I cannot now confess to Thy minister in the holy Sacrament of Penance, I desire to confess my sins to Thee. I humbly beg of Thee to restore the priesthood to Thy Church, so that I can once again confess to Thy minister as Thou willest. I offer all of my efforts, prayers and penance and consecrate myself to do all in my power to bring about the restoration of the priesthood for the salvation of souls and my own salvation. But, O my God, how miserably shall I deceive myself if Thou assist me not in this great work by Thy heavenly light. O then remove every veil that hides any of my sins from me, that I may see them all in their true colors, and may sincerely detest them. O let me no longer be imposed upon by the Enemy of souls, or by my own self-centeredness, so as to mistake vice for virtue, or in any way to make excuses for my sins.

But, O my good God, what will it avail me to know my sins, if Thou dost not also give me a hearty sorrow and repentance for them? Without this my sins will be all upon me still, and I shall be still Thine enemy and a child of hell. Thou dost require that a contrite heart, without which there can be no reconciliation with Thee; and this heart none but Thyself can give. O then, dear Lord, grant it unto me at this time. Give me a lively faith, and a steadfast hope, in the Passion of my Redeemer; teach me to fear Thee and to love Thee. Give me, for Thy mercy's sake, a hearty sorrow for having offended so good a God. Teach me to detest my evil ways; to abhor all my past ingratitude; to have in myself now with a perfect hatred for my many treasons against Thee. O give me a full and firm resolution to lead henceforward a new life; and to unite me unto Thee with an eternal band of love which nothing in life or death may ever break.

Grant me also the grace to make an entire and sincere confession of all my sins, and to accept the confusion of it as a penance justly due to my transgressions. Let not the Enemy prevail upon me to pass over anything through fear or shame; rather let me die than to consent to so great an evil. Let no self-love deceive me, as I fear it has done too often. O grant that this confession may be good; and for the sake of Jesus Christ, Thy Son, Who died for me and for all sinners, assist me in every part of my preparation for it; that I may perform it with the same care and diligence as I should be glad to do at the hour of my death; that so, being perfectly reconciled to Thee, I may never offend Thee again. Amen.

Prayer Before Examination of Conscience

O Almighty God, Maker of heaven and earth, King of kings, and Lord of lords, Who hast made me out of nothing in Thine image and likeness, and hast redeemed me with Thine own Blood; whom I a sinner am not worthy to name or call upon Thee; I humbly pray Thee, I earnestly beseech Thee, to look mercifully on me, Thy wicked servant. Thou Who had mercy on the woman of Chanaan and Mary Magdalene; Thou Who didst spare the publican and the thief upon the cross, have mercy upon me. Thou art my hope and my trust; my guide and my succor; my comfort and my strength; my defense and my deliverance; my life, my health, and my resurrection; my light and my longing; my help and my protection. I pray and entreat Thee, help me and I shall be safe; direct me and defend me; strengthen me and comfort me; confirm me and gladden me; enlighten me and come unto me. Raise me from the dead; I am Thy creature, and the work of Thy hands. Despise me not, O Lord, nor regard my iniquities; but according to the multitude of Thy tender mercies have mercy upon me, the chief of sinners, and be gracious to me. Turn Thou unto me, O Lord, and be not angry with me. I implore Thee, most compassionate Father, I pray Thee meekly, of Thy great mercy, to bring me to a holy death, and to true penance, to a perfect confession, and to worthy satisfaction for all my sins. Amen.

O Lord God, Who enlightens every man who comes into this world, enlighten my heart, I pray Thee, with the light of Thy grace, that I may fully know my sins, shortcomings, and negligences, and may confess them with that true sorrow and contrition of heart which I so much need. I desire to make full amends for all my sins and to avoid them for the future for Thy honor and glory, and for the salvation of my soul, through Jesus Christ our Lord. Amen.

I believe in Thee, O God, Father, Son, and Holy Ghost, my Creator, my Redeemer, and my Sanctifier; I believe that Thou art all-holy, just, and merciful. I believe that Thou art willing to pardon and save me, if I repent and forsake my sins. O my God, strengthen and increase my faith, and grant me the grace of a true repentance, for Jesus Christ's sake. Amen.

I hope in Thee, O my God, because Thou art almighty, faithful, and long-suffering. I humbly trust that Thou wilt pardon my sins for the sake of Thy dear Son Jesus Christ, Who suffered and died for me upon the Cross; and that Thou will cleanse my sinful soul in His precious Blood and make me holy, and bring me safe to everlasting life.

O Lord, in Thee have I hoped, let me never be confounded. Amen.

I Love Thee, O my God, above all things, because Thou hast been so good, so patient, and so loving to me, notwithstanding all the sins by which I have so grievously offended Thee. I love Thee, O Blessed Jesus, my Saviour, because Thou did suffer so much for love of me, an ungrateful sinner, and did die on the Cross for my salvation.

O make me love Thee more and more, and show my love to Thee by faithfully keeping Thy Commandments all the days of my life. Amen.

O Mary Immaculate, Mother of Fair Love; obtain for me that love of God, which is so necessary for true contrition. Amen.

O Lord, help me to remember my sins, so that I can be sorry for them and root out their cause and resolve to sin no more. R/Amen.

Examination of Conscience

These are the commandments which God gave to man to guide him to happiness in this life and in the next:

I. I Am The Lord Thy God: Thou Shalt Not Have Strange Gods Before Me. Commands: faith, hope, love, and worship of God; reverence for holy things; prayer. Forbids: idolatry, superstition, spiritism, tempting God, sacrilege, attendance at false worship.

II. Thou Shalt Not Take The Name Of The Lord Thy God In Vain. Commands: reverence in speaking about God and holy things; the keeping of oaths and vows. Forbids: blasphemy, the irreverent use of God's name, speaking disrespectfully of holy things, false oaths, and the breaking of vows.

III. Remember Thou Keep Holy The Sabbath Day. Commands: going to Church on Sundays and holy days, keeping the day holy by prayer, Holy Hour, spiritual reading, studying catechism and instructing one's family in the catechism. Forbids: missing Church through one's own fault; unnecessary servile work; public buying and selling; court trials.

IV. Honor Thy Father And Mother. Commands: love, respect, obedience on the part of children; care on the part of parents for the spiritual and temporal welfare of their children; obedience to civil and religious superiors. Forbids: hatred of parents and superiors; disrespect, disobedience.

V. Thou Shalt Not Kill. Commands: safeguarding of one's own life and bodily welfare and that of others. Forbids: unjust killing, suicide, abortion sterilization, dueling, endangering life and limb of self or others. Anger and gluttony are also forbidden by this Commandment.

VI. Thou Shalt Not Commit Adultery. Commands: chastity in word, and deed. Forbids: obscene speech; impure actions alone or with others.

VII. Thou Shalt Not Steal. Commands: respect for the property and rights of others; the paying of just debts; paying just wages to employees; integrity in public officials. Forbids: theft; damage to the property of others; not paying just debts; not returning found or borrowed articles; giving unjust measure or weight in selling; not paying just wages; bribery; graft; cheating; fraud; accepting stolen property; not giving an honest day's work for wages received; violation of contract, usury.

VIII. Thou Shalt Not Bear False Witness Against Thy Neighbor. Commands: truthfulness, respect for the good name of others; the observance of secrecy when required. Forbids: lying, injury to the good name of others, slander; talebearing, rash judgment, contemptuous speech, and the violation of secrecy. Calumny and detraction are also forbidden by this Commandment.

IX. Thou Shalt Not Covet Thy Neighbor's Wife. Commands: purity in thought. Forbids: willful impure thoughts and desires.

X. Thou Shalt Not Covet Thy Neighbor's Goods. Commands: respect for the rights of others. Forbids: the desire to take, to keep, or to damage the property of others.

The Seven Deadly Sins: Pride, Covetousness, Lust, Anger, Gluttony, Envy, Sloth.

Commandments of the Church

1. To hear Mass on Sundays and holydays of obligation.
2. To fast and abstain on the days appointed.
3. To confess at least once a year.
4. To receive the Holy Eucharist during the Eastertime.
5. To contribute to the support of the Church.

6. Not to marry persons who are not Catholics, or who are related to us within the third degree of kindred, nor privately without witnesses, nor to solemnize marriage at forbidden times.

7. To learn the truths of the Faith.

There are nine ways to cooperate in the sin of another: Counsel, command, consent, provocation, praise or flattery, concealment, partaking, silence, or defense of the ill-done.

Final consideration: How much have I done to overcome my own *pet sin*, that is the sin I am most prone to commit? What sin did I specifically resolve last week to work on eradicating? How well have I done? What sin shall I work on next week? O God, give me the grace to eliminate sin from my life.

Prayer After Examination of Conscience

O My God, I cry unto Thee with the prodigal son: Father, I have sinned against heaven and before Thee; I am no longer worthy to be called Thy Son.

I have gone astray like a sheep that is lost. O seek Thy servant, for I have not forgotten Thy commandments.

Enter not into judgment with Thy servant, O Lord. O spare me for Thy mercy's sake.

Prove me, O God, and know my heart; examine me, and know my paths.

Thou Whose property is always to have mercy and to spare, O meet me in pity, embrace me in love, and forgive me all my sin.

I confess my sins unto Thee, O Christ, Healer of our souls, O Lord of Life. Heal me, heal me of my spiritual sickness, Thou Who art long-suffering and of tender mercy; heal me, O Lord Christ.

Accept my supplications, O Thou Holy Ghost, unto Whom every heart is open, every desire is known, and from Whom no secret is hidden, and Who gives life to our souls; hear and answer, O Spirit of God.

O Heavenly Father, Who wills not that any sinner should perish, give me true repentance for my sins, that I do not perish!

To what misery am I come by my own fault! O merciful God, pity and forgive me for Jesus' sake.

Thine eyes, O God, are as flames of fire searching my inmost heart. O pardon my sin, for it is great!

Thou, God, seest me in all the foulness of my sins! Blessed Jesus, speak for me, plead for me, come between my soul and my offended God, that I perish not. Amen.

Prayer Before Confession

Accept my confession, O most loving, most gracious Lord Jesus Christ, on Whom alone my soul trusts for salvation. Grant me, I bessech Thee, contrition of heart, and give tears to my eyes, that I may sorrow deeply for all my sins with humility and sincerity of heart.

O good Jesus, Saviour of the world, Who gave Thyself to the death of the Cross to save sinners, look on me, a miserable sinner who calls upon Thy Name. Spare me, Thou Who are my Saviour, and pity my sinful soul; loose its chains, heal its sores. Lord Jesus, I desire Thee, I seek Thee, I long for Thee; show me the light of Thy countenance, and I shall be saved; send forth Thy light and Thy truth into my soul, to show me fully all the sins and shortcomings which I must still confess, and to aid and teach me to lay them bare without reserve and with a contrite heart; O Thou Who lives and reigns with God the Father, in the unity of the Holy Ghost, one God, world without end. Amen.

O most gracious Virgin Mary, beloved Mother of Jesus Christ, my Redeemer, intercede for me with Him. Obtain for me the full remission of my sins, and perfect amendment of life, to the salvation of my soul and the glory of His Name. Amen.

I implore the same grace of thee, O my Angel Guardian; of you, my holy Patrons, *insert their name(s) here*; of you, O blessed Peter and holy Magdalene, and of all the Saints of God. Intercede for me a sinner, repenting of my sins, firmly resolving to confess them as soon as this is possible, consecrating myself to bring this day closer, and firmly resolving to avoid my sins and the near occasion of committing them in the future with the help of Almighty God. Amen.

Here Confess Your Sins to God Just As You Would to a Priest

Act of Perfect Contrition

My God, because Thou art infinite goodness, I love Thee above all things, and because I love Thee above all things I am sorry for the offences I have offered to Thee, O Sovereign God! My God, I purpose never more to offend Thee. I would rather die than offend Thee more.

O my God, I resolve with the help of Thy grace to avoid sin and the near occasions of sin. Amen.

O God, Who doesn't reject anyone that comes unto Thee, but in pity are appeased even with the greatest sinners who repent, mercifully regard our prayers in our humiliation, and lighten our hearts, that we may be able to fulfill Thy commandments. Through Christ our Lord. Amen.

Thanksgiving After Confession

O Most merciful God, Who according to the multitude of Thy mercies dost so put away the sins of those who truly repent that Thou remember them no more: look graciously upon me, Thine unworthy servant, and accept my confession for Thy mercy's sake; receive my humble thanks, most loving Father, that of Thy great goodness Thou hast given me pardon for all my sins. O may Thy love and pity supply whatsoever has been wanting in the sufficiency of my contrition, and the fullness of my confession. Help to be able to one day confess to Thy minister as Thou willest and to consecrate myself to bring this day closer and dedicate my life to Thee. And do Thou, O Lord, vouchsafe to grant me the help of Thy grace, that I may diligently amend my life and persevere in Thy service unto the end, through Jesus Christ our Lord. Amen.

Perfect Act of Contrition

There are two types of contrition, perfect and imperfect. The common Act of Contrition contains both:

O My God, I am heartily sorry for having offended Thee. I detest all of my sins, because I dread the loss of heaven and the pains of hell, but most of all, because they offend Thee, Almighty God, Who art all good and deserving of all my love. I firmly resolve with the help of Thy grace to confess my sins, do penance and amend my life. Amen.

Imperfect contrition, which is also called attrition, is a hatred of sin because of the punishment it deserves. "I detest all of my sins, because I dread the loss of heaven and the pains of hell" expresses imperfect contrition. This is sufficient for the Sacrament of Confession.

Perfect Contrition is a hatred of sin, because it is an offense against the infinitely good God. This is expressed by the words, "but most of all, because they offend Thee, Almighty God, Who art all good and deserving of all my love." This is required for the Perfect Act of Contrition, which we should make immediately after committing mortal sin. This perfect act of contrition contains a desire to confess our sins to a duly authorized priest as soon as possible, as Saint Thomas Aquinas teaches. This is sufficient to restore the state of grace until we can make an actual confession. However, this does not make one fit to receive Holy Communion. For this we must have confessed and been absolved of all of our mortal sins.

Perfect Contrition Prayer

My God, because Thou art infinite goodness, I love Thee above all things, and because I love Thee above all things I am sorry for the offences I have offered to Thee, O Sovereign God! My God, I purpose never more to offend Thee. I would rather die than offend Thee more.

O my God, I resolve with the help of Thy grace to avoid sin and the near occasions of sin. Amen.

O God, Who doesn't reject anyone that comes unto Thee, but in pity are appeased even with the greatest sinners who repent, mercifully regard our prayers in our humiliation, and lighten our hearts, that we may be able to fulfill Thy commandments. Through Christ our Lord. Amen.

Saint John Eudes on Confession

Preparation For Confession

The frequent use of the Sacrament of Penance is a very useful, holy and necessary means for the glory of God and the sanctification of souls.

But it is a deplorable thing to see what a strange abuse many souls make of this Sacrament in our own day, when they come to the feet of the priest to receive absolution for their sins, but get up and bear away their own condemnation because they have come without the dispositions necessary for true and solid repentance. This is a matter to be feared extremely, even by those who confess frequently, because there is a real danger of their going to confession more as a matter of routine than in a real spirit of penance, especially when they can detect no change in their life and no progress in Christian virtues. Therefore, the more you frequent this Sacrament, the more you should see that you make the proper preparation for receiving it. There are three things that will enable you to do so.

I. You must fall on your knees before Our Lord, in some quiet place, if possible, to consider Him and adore Him in the rigorous penances, in the contrition and humiliation which He had to bear for your sins all through His life, especially in the Garden of Olives. And you should beg Him with great insistence to let you share in His spirit of penance, and to give you the grace to know your sins, to hate and detest them as much as He would wish, to confess them clearly, and to give them up absolutely and to be converted perfectly to Him, flying from all occasions of sin, while making use of the remedies necessary for the healing of the wounds of your soul.

To do this, you may use the following prayer:

O my dear Jesus, as I contemplate Thee in the Garden of Olives when Thou didst enter upon Thy Sacred Passion, I behold Thee prostrate upon the ground before Thy Father's face in the name of all sinners, since Thou hast taken upon Thyself all the sins of the world and, especially, my own. I see that by Thy divine light Thou dost place all those sins before Thy own gaze, to confess them to Thy Father in the name of all sinners, taking upon Thyself all the humiliation and contrition for them in His sight, and offering Thyself to Him to make whatever satisfaction and perform whatever penance is pleasing to Him.

O my Good Jesus, I behold Thee, as a result of this spectacle of the horror of my crimes and of the dishonor they give to Thy Father, reduced to an astounding agony, a frightful sorrow and to such an extremity of anguish and contrition, that the violence of the suffering makes Thy soul sorrowful unto death and causes Thee even to sweat blood, so terribly as to stain the ground about Thee.

O my Saviour, I adore, love and glorify Thee in Thy holy agony and in this spirit of penance to which Thou hast been reduced by Thy love and my offenses. I give myself to Thee now, that I may enter with Thee into this spirit. May it please Thee to give me some little share of the light that gave Thee cognizance of my faults, that I may know them and confess them humbly. Give me some small share of the humiliation and contrition Thou didst bear before the Eternal Father, as well as some measure of the love with which Thou didst offer Thyself to Him in atonement and some fraction of Thy hatred and horror for sin. Give me the grace, I beseech Thee, to make this confession with perfect humility, sincerity and repentance and with a firm and strong resolution never to offend Thee again.

O Mother of Jesus, I implore thee to obtain for me those graces from thy Son.

O my holy guardian Angel, pray to Our Lord for me, to give me the grace to know my sins and confess them well, and to have true contrition for them and to be perfectly converted from them.

2. When you have said this prayer, you should examine your conscience with care and try to remember the sins you have committed since your last confession. Once you have recognized them, try to form in your heart real regret, perfect repentance and contrition for having offended so good a God, asking Him pardon for your faults, detesting them and renouncing them because they displease Him, making a firm resolution to avoid them in the future, with the help of His grace, flying from all occasions of sin, and making use of the proper and efficacious means to bring about a genuine conversion: for contrition is composed of all these elements.

Since, however, contrition is extremely necessary and important, not only in confession but in several other matters as well, I should like to show you in more detail the nature of contrition, and when and how you ought to make acts of contrition. This will be done after I have told you the third thing necessary for a perfect confession and what to do after you have confessed.

3. The third thing you must do, if you want to make a perfect confession, is to kneel before the priest as before one who represents the Person of Jesus Christ and takes His place. Present yourself to him as a criminal who has outraged the majesty of God, with the full intention of humiliating and confounding yourself, taking God's side against yourself, as against His enemy which you are in so far as you are a sinner, and being ready to arm yourself with His zeal for justice against sin and His infinite hatred for it. Do not fail to bring with you the firm resolve to confess your sins humbly, completely and clearly, without disguises, without excuses, and without trying to shift the blame on to somebody else. But rather accuse yourself as though you were on the point of death. For it would be well to reflect that it is far better to state your sins in the ear of the priest than to bear the shame of them on the day of judgment, before the entire world, and then be damned forever.

Remember that you ought to be willing to accept with cheerfulness and courage the pain and confusion that go with the confession of sins, out of homage for the confusion and torments suffered by our Lord Jesus Christ upon the Cross for those very same sins, as well as to glorify Our Lord by your humiliations, remembering that the more you abase yourself, the more He is exalted in you.

Thanksgiving After Confession

After you have confessed your sins and received pardon for them through the Sacrament of Penance, do not forget to thank Our Lord for having given you so great a grace. When He delivers you from some great sin, either by preventing you from falling into it, or by pardoning you after your fall, even if it is only the smallest venial sin in the world, He is giving you a greater grace, for which you owe Him more thanks, than if He had preserved you from all the plagues, diseases and other afflictions of the body that might beset you. Therefore, thank Him in such words as these, praying Him to preserve you from sin in the future.

Be Thou blessed, O Good Jesus, be Thou blessed a thousand times! May all Thy angels and Thy saints and Thy holy Mother bless Thee now and forever, for having established in Thy Church the holy Sacrament of Penance and for having given us so accessible, so easy and so efficacious a means of wiping out our sins and becoming reconciled with Thee! Be Thou blessed for all the glory that has been and will be given Thee by this sacrament until the end of the world! Blessed be Thou, also, for all the glory Thou hast Thyself rendered to Thy Father by the confession, if one may say such a thing, which Thou didst make to Him of our sins, in the Garden of Olives and by the humiliation, contrition and penance Thou didst bear for them! O my Saviour, engrave deep within me a great hatred, abhorrence and fear of sin, greater than all the other evils on earth and in hell and let me die a thousand deaths rather than offend Thee again.

Nature Of Contrition

Contrition is so powerful, so holy and so desirable that a single act of true contrition is capable of wiping out a thousand mortal sins, if they were to be found in the soul.

Contrition is an act of hatred and abhorrence, of sorrow and repentance at the sight of a sin you have committed, because this sin offends God. It is an act of the will, by which you tell God that you desire to hate and detest your sins, that you are filled with shame for having committed them, and that you renounce them earnestly, not for your own interests but because of His. By this I mean, not so much because of the evil, injury and harm you have done to yourself, as because of the dishonor, great sufferings and most cruel death you have caused Our Lord to suffer by your sins.

It is true that the very slightest offense against the infinite goodness of God is so detestable that even if you were to weep until the day of judgment, or even if you were to die of grief over the smallest of your faults, it would not be enough. Nevertheless, in order to have contrition it is not absolutely necessary to shed tears, nor to conceive a pain that can be felt, nor a sensible feeling of anguish over our sins. Contrition is an interior and spiritual act of the will which is a spiritual power and not a faculty of sense; therefore, you may make an act of contrition without any sensible pain. It is enough to assure Our Lord, with the real will to carry out what you promise, that you want to hate and detest your sins and to avoid them in future, because they displease Him, and that you shall confess them at your next confession.

It should also be remembered that contrition is a gift of God and an effect of grace. Even if you had perfect knowledge of its essence and applied all the strength of your mind and will to make an act of contrition, you would never be able to do so if the Holy Ghost did not give you grace. But you may console yourself with the thought that this grace will never be refused if you ask for it with humility, confidence and perseverance, and if you do not wait until the hour of your death to ask for it. For grace is ordinarily refused, in that last hour, to those who have neglected it during their lifetime.

Notice, also, that four things are necessary for true contrition. The first of these is to make restitution, at the earliest possible opportunity of things belonging to others, if you have anything that it is possible to return; also to restore the good name of another when you have robbed him of it by calumny or backbiting.

The second thing is to do everything in your power to bring about reconciliation with those with whom you are at odds.

The third is to have a firm and constant will, not only to confess your sins and renounce them, but also to use the necessary remedies and means to overcome evil habits, and to begin to live a truly Christian life.

The fourth thing is effectively to give up all active and passive occasions of sin—that is, the occasions you give others to offend God, as well as those by which you yourself are led into sin.

Such occasions are, for instance: for the promiscuously impure and the adulterous, their partners in evil; for drunkards, their taverns; for gamblers and blasphemers, their games, when they have the habit of swearing and blaspheming or losing very much time and money at these pastimes; women and girls should avoid the least thing that tends to immodesty in dress, as well as excessive novelty and vanity in the matter of fashions; others should give up bad books, improper pictures, the wrong kind of parties and shows, and avoid certain groups, or certain individuals, as well as certain occupations which lead them into sin.

The Son of God Himself says: "If thy hand, or thy foot scandalize thee, cut it off, and cast it from thee. It is better for thee to go into life maimed or lame, than having two hands or two feet, to be cast into hell fire. And if thy eye scandalize thee, pluck it out, and cast it from thee. It is better for thee having one eye to enter into life, than having two eyes to be cast into hell fire" (Matt. 18, 8-9). He is giving you here an absolute commandment under pain of eternal damnation (as the holy Fathers explain these words of Sacred Scripture), to cut off from yourself and entirely renounce all things that are occasions of ruin for yourself and others, even those which are not in themselves evil, even occupations and professions, if you cannot follow them without sinning, as well as things that are most close and dear and precious to you, if these things might occasion the loss of your soul.

Acts of contrition may be made at all times and in every situation, but they should be made particularly at such times as:

I. When you go to confession, for perfect contrition or at the very least attrition, which is imperfect contrition, is a necessary part of Penance. That is why I said above and here repeat, that, before you go to confession and after your examination of conscience, you should ask God for contrition and then try to make genuine acts of sorrow for sin.

2. When you have fallen into sin, so that you may instantly rise again by means of contrition.

3. In the morning and evening, so that if you have committed any sins during the night or in the day, they may be wiped out by contrition, and so you may always keep in God's grace. For this cause I have set down various acts of contrition in the evening exercise, following the examination of conscience.

But over and above this, to give you readier access to the means and method of practicing so necessary and important a virtue, which you need at every moment of your life, I have also added several varied acts of contrition which you may use, taking now one, now another, according to the promptings and guidance of the Spirit of God.

But do not make the mistake of imagining that, in order to have contrition for your sins, it is sufficient to read and pronounce with attention the acts set down in this book, or others like them. True contrition must be accompanied by the conditions described above, but you must also remember in particular that you can not make a single act of contrition without a special grace from God. Therefore, when you want to have true repentance and contrition for your faults, be sure to pray Our Lord to give you grace to do so.

Prayer To Beg God For Contrition

O Good Jesus, I desire to have all the contrition and repentance for my faults that Thou desirest me to have. Yet Thou dost know that I can not have this unless Thou dost give it to me. Grant me contrition, I beg Thee, O my Saviour, in Thy great mercy. I know that I am unworthy that Thou shouldst look upon me and hear my prayer, but I trust in Thy infinite bounty, believing that Thou wilt give me what I ask of Thee most fervently, through the merits of Thy holy passion, of Thy holy Mother and of all Thy angels and saints.

O Mother of Jesus, O holy angels and blessed saints, pray to Jesus for me that He may give me perfect repentance for my sins.

After this prayer strive to make earnest acts of pure contrition:

Acts Of Contrition

O my Most Amiable Jesus, I hate and detest my sins for love of Thee.

O my Saviour, I renounce all sin forever because it offends Thee.

O my Jesus, I abhor my offenses because of the insult and dishonor I have given Thee by them.

O my God, would that I had never offended Thee, for Thou art so worthy of honor and love.

O my Lord, I desire to have all the contrition Thou dost will me to have for my sins.

O my God, would that I had in my heart all the sorrow and contrition possessed by all the penitent saints.

O Good Jesus, make me share the sorrow which Thou Thyself didst bear for my sins. I desire to have the greatest possible measure of the same contrition that Thou didst bear.

O Father of Jesus, I offer up to Thee and unite myself with the contrition and penance that Thy Well-beloved Son did feel for my sins.

O Most Amiable Jesus, may I hate and detest my sins because they were the cause of Thy torments and Thy dreadful death on the Cross.

O my God, I want to hate my sins as vehemently as Thy angels and saints hate them.

O my God, I desire to hate and detest my sins with the same hatred with which Thou dost hate and detest them Thyself.

You might also make an act of contrition by striking your breast like the poor publican in the Gospel and saying with him: "O God, be merciful to me a sinner" (Luke 18, 13). But you must desire to do and say this with the same contrition that the publican had, by virtue of which he went down to his house justified, as we are told by the Son of God Himself.

These are a few acts of contrition, which are capable of wiping out all sorts of sins, provided only that they be uttered, either with the lips or in the heart, with a real will prompted by the workings of grace, and with a firm resolve to abandon sin and the occasions of sin, and to confess it, and carry out [at the earliest possible opportunity] all the other conditions mentioned above.

Saint Alphonsus on Confession

Act before Confession

O God of infinite majesty, behold at Thy feet a traitor, who has offended Thee over and over again, but who now humbly seeks forgiveness. O Lord, reject me not; Thou dost not despise a heart that humbles itself: A contrite and humbled heart, O God, Thou wilt not despise. I thank Thee that Thou hast waited for me till now, and has not let me die in sin, casting me into hell, as I deserved. Since Thou hast waited for me, my God. I hope that, by the merits of Jesus Christ, Thou wilt pardon me in this confession for all the offences I have committed against Thee; I repent, and am sorry for them, because by them I have merited hell and lost paradise. But above all, it is not so much. on account of hell which I have merited, but because I have offended Thee, O Infinite Goodness! that I am sorry from the bottom of my heart. I love Thee, O Sovereign Good! and because I love Thee, I repent of all the insults I have offered Thee. I have turned my back upon Thee; I have not respected Thee; I have despised Thy grace and Thy friendship. O Lord! I have lost Thee by my own free-will; forgive me all my sins for the love of Jesus Christ, now that I repent with all my heart; I hate, detest, and abominate them above every evil. And I repent not only of mortal sins, but also of venial sins, because these are also displeasing to Thee. I resolve for the future, by Thy grace, never more willfully to offend Thee. Yes, my God, I will rather die than ever sin again.

And if a person confesses a sin into which he has often relapsed, it is a good thing to resolve particularly not to fall into it again, by promising to avoid the occasion of it, and to take the means pointed out by the confessor, or such as he may himself judge to be most efficacious for correcting himself of it.

Act after Confession

My dear Jesus! how much do I not owe Thee: By the merits of Thy blood I hope that I have this day been pardoned. I thank Thee above all things. I hope to reach heaven, where I shall praise Thy mercies forever. My God, if I have hitherto lost Thee so often, I now desire to lose Thee no more. From this day forward I will change my life in earnest. Thou dost merit all my love; I will love Thee truly; I will no longer see myself separated from Thee. I have promised Thee this already; now I repeat my promise of being ready to die rather than offend Thee again. I promise also to avoid all occasions of sin, and to use such means as will prevent me from falling again. My Jesus, Thou knowest my weakness: give me grace to be faithful to Thee till death, and to have recourse to Thee when I am tempted. Most holy Mary, help me! Thou art the mother of perseverance; I place my hope in thee.

Various Prayers

Saint Alphonsus says of the following prayer, "Whenever you will have said this prayer, with the requisite determination of avoiding all sin, go in peace to confession, without scruple and without fear."

O my God, I love Thee above all things. I hope, by the merits and Passion of Jesus Christ, to obtain pardon of my sins. I grieve from the bottom of my heart for having by them offended Thy infinite goodness. I detest them more than all imaginable evils. I unite my grief for them to that by which Jesus Christ was oppressed in the Garden of Olives. I firmly resolve, by the assistance of Thy grace, nevermore to offend Thee. Amen.

Prayer to the Holy Ghost before Confession: Come, Holy Ghost, enlighten my mind and inflame my heart, so that I may confess my sins worthily, and, being truly penitent, may amend my life, and henceforth serve Thee faithfully and glorify Thee with all the powers of my soul and of my body. Amen.

Saint Mechtild's Act of Contrition: O sweet Jesus, I grieve for my sins; vouchsafe to supply whatever is lacking to my true sorrow, and to offer for me to God the Father all the grief which Thou hast endured because of my sins and those of the whole world. Amen.

Act of Sorrow: My dear Lord and Savior, my sins have fastened Thee to this Cross. I know it is just as if I had myself fixed the crown of thorns upon Thy brow; as if, with my own hands, I had driven the nails through Thy sacred hands and feet. O my sweet Jesus, I did not know that I was doing in committing these sins, I did not think, but I see it all now. I have truck and wounded and insulted Thee. I am sorry for all my sins. Forgive me, dear Lord; I will confess them now, and I firmly resolve with Thy help, never to commit them again. Amen.

Basic Act of Contrition

O My God, I am heartily sorry for having offended Thee. I detest all of my sins, because I dread the loss of heaven and the pains of hell, but most of all, because they offend Thee, Almighty God, Who art all good and deserving of all my love. I firmly resolve with the help of Thy grace to confess my sins, do penance and amend my life. Amen.

Perfect Act of Contrition

My God, because Thou art infinite goodness, I love Thee above all things, and because I love Thee above all things I am sorry for the offences I have offered to Thee, O Sovereign God! My God, I purpose never more to offend Thee. I would rather die than offend Thee more.

O my God, I resolve with the help of Thy grace to avoid sin and the near occasions of sin. Amen.

O God, Who doesn't reject anyone that comes unto Thee, but in pity are appeased even with the greatest sinners who repent, mercifully regard our prayers in our humiliation, and lighten our hearts, that we may be able to fulfill Thy commandments. Through Christ our Lord. Amen.

From Saint Pius X Press

Beauty A Study In Philosophy
Bernadette Of Lourdes The Only Complete Account Of Her Life Ever Published
Characteristics Of True Devotion
Conference Matter For Religious
Eternal Punishment
Holiness Of Life
Holy Week Manual For Servers
Mercy Is Forever
New Lights On Pastoral Problems
Peter's Name
Practical Method Of Reading The Breviary
Readings For Each Sunday In The Year
Readings On Fundamental Moral Theology
Sanctity In America
Sister Faustina: Apostle Of Divine Mercy
Spiritual Maxims
The Art Of Dying Well
The Art Of Prayer
The Blessed Sacrament: The Centre of Immutable Truth
The Christian Trumpet
The Cult of Our Lady
The Divine Office
The Four Temperaments
The Mirror Of The Blessed Virgin Mary And The Psalter Of Our Lady
The Pastoral Office
The Possibility Of Invincible Ignorance Of The Natural Law
The Precepts Of The Church
The Present Crisis Of The Holy See
The Religious State
The True Story Of The Vatican Council
The Virtues Of A Religious Superior
Vocations

'Layman's Guide to Perfection' is an excellent book for anyone who wants to save their soul. Written in the Twentieth Century, this work gives simple to understand instructions in achieving perfection, which is reuiqred to enter heaven.

'The Art of Prayer' also from the Twentieth Century is most likely the most comprehensive work on acquiring the habit of prayer and beginning the spiritual life.

We also recommend 'The Four Temperaments' as a guide to finding one's weaknesses and strengths in the spiritual life.

'The Precepts of the Church' is the only work to our knowledge on the Commandments of the Church, although these are discussed in Cardinal Gasparri's Catechism and all basic Catechisms.

We recommend visiting the website or ordering a catalog for a complete list of titles currently available.

Saint Pius X Press
Box 74
Delia KS 66418
www.stpiusxpress.com
contact@stpiusxpress.com

Made in the USA
Columbia, SC
26 January 2020